SEO A Comprehensive Guide

Nishant Baxi

ISBN 978-93-5883-094-1
© Nishant Baxi 2023

Published in India 2023 by Pencil

A brand of
One Point Six Technologies Pvt. Ltd.
Unit no. 26, Ground Floor, Building A1,
Wadala Truck Terminal Road,
Near Post Office, Antop Hill, Mumbai - 400037
E connect@thepencilapp.com
W www.thepencilapp.com

Author biography

I am an experienced content creator and digital/social media marketing professional with a demonstrated history of working in the publishing industry. I am skilled in E-Learning, Market Research, Online Advertising, Management, and Business Development, Content Development.

CONTENTS

Introduction

Overview of Search Engine Optimization (SEO)
Search Engine Optimization, commonly known as SEO, constitutes a fundamental component of digital marketing strategies. With the rapid evolution of Internet technology and digital media, businesses utilize SEO's power to boost their online visibility and reach their potential customers more efficiently (Moz, 2020). Understanding the concept and main components of SEO is, therefore, pivotal for businesses seeking to establish a robust online presence.

SEO refers to strategies aimed at enhancing a website's visibility on search engine result pages (SERPs). When done correctly, SEO can improve the quality and quantity of website traffic, organically - an activity implying unpaid appearance in the SERPs (Google, 2021). A primary objective of SEO includes employing techniques aligned with the algorithms of search engines to rank a website higher in search results.

The main components of SEO encompass on-page SEO, off-page SEO, and technical SEO (Forbes, 2017). On-page SEO relates to optimizing individual web pages for specific keywords. This technique involves the creation of high-quality content, optimizing the HTML source code, keyword placement, and usage. On the other hand, off-page SEO includes actions taken outside the website to raise its ranking on the SERPs. Fundamental tactics in this sphere involve backlinks creation from high-authority websites. Lastly, technical SEO concentrates on the non-content elements of a website. It includes website speed, mobile-friendliness, indexing, crawlability, site architecture, structured data, and security.

SEO offers numerous benefits to businesses. One is driving quality traffic to websites. Unlike traditional marketing strategies, SEO is an inbound marketing strategy, which makes it customer-centric. This approach helps companies attract prospects who are actively seeking information related to their business or industry (HubSpot, 2021). Besides, SEO provides businesses a competitive advantage. Web pages appearing higher in search results organically are likely to receive more clicks, increasing the chances of converting prospects into customers.

However, achieving higher rankings on SERPs requires a balance among various components of SEO, accompanied by an understanding of search engine algorithms' changing dynamics. Owing to regular updates in algorithms by search engines like Google, SEO demands constant tracking and adjustment of optimization strategies. All these considerations have prompted more businesses to invest in professional SEO services, ensuring their websites maintain an optimal online presence.

In conclusion, SEO proves to be an indispensable digital marketing instrument in the current era. It not only improves the quantity and quality of traffic towards websites but also offers a competitive edge in the increasingly crowded online marketplace. Therefore, understanding SEO's basic principles and components, maintaining an up-to-date knowledge of algorithm changes, and crafting a balanced optimization strategy in place, are essential for businesses to capitalize on their online endeavors.

The Importance of SEO

The competitive landscape of online businesses continually evolves, and the advent of SEO, or Search Engine Optimization, has played a significant role in this evolution. SEO is a digital marketing strategy that aims to increase website visibility through organic search engine results, thus driving more traffic to your website (Patel, 2020). It has become an essential part of digital marketing due to its myriad of benefits.

Firstly, SEO helps to improve a website's visibility amongst its target audience. Studies illustrate that the majority of web users utilize search engines to find information on the internet (Purcell, Brenner, & Raine, 2012). This means that if a website ranks highly on search engine rankings, it is more likely to get noticed.

Secondly, SEO not only makes a website more accessible but also enhances the user's experience. By employing strategic keywords, relevant metadata, and easy-to-navigate site maps, SEO improves website usability, making it more intuitive and user-friendly (Enge, Spencer, Stricchiola, & Fishkin, 2012).

Moreover, SEO can influence the buying cycle positively. SEO-optimized websites provide valuable and up-to-date content that helps potential customers make informed decisions. By offering the required insights, businesses build trust and credibility with their audience, improving their chances of making sales (Google, 2021).

Finally, SEO provides a comparatively cost-effective strategy compared to other forms of online advertising like PPC advertising or purchasing leads for an email marketing program (Fishkin, 2013). Its inbound nature aids businesses to save money as opposed to outbound strategies that require more funding.

As the digital marketplace continues to grow, the implementation of SEO becomes increasingly important for businesses seeking to survive and thrive in the competitive online environment. For heightened visibility, improved user experience, a better buying cycle, and cost-effectiveness, integrating SEO into your digital marketing strategy is imperative.

Objectives of The Book

The fundamental focus of any online business is to capture as much traffic as possible, and one of the quintessential ways of achieving this is through implementing Search Engine Optimization (SEO) strategies. The objective of this chapter is to provide a comprehensive guide to understanding SEO, as encapsulated in the theoretical framework of a hypothetical book titled "SEO: A Comprehensive Guide."

Search Engine Optimization (SEO) is a critical digital marketing discipline that focuses on improving website visibility in organic (non-paid) search engine result pages (SERPs), thus driving website traffic and potential conversions. This traffic is often of high quality, as the visitors are typically actively looking for the products, services, or information that the website offers (Rognerud, 2018). With this backdrop, the significance of an insightful conceptual book on SEO that delivers a comprehensive and systematic overview of the subject can't be understated.

The primary objectives of the book "SEO: A Comprehensive Guide" would lie in equipping its readers with a broad and deep understanding of the different components of SEO, the strategies involved, common challenges, future trends, and practical case studies. It expects to achieve this by presenting complex SEO concepts in a format that's easily digestible for both SEO novices and seasoned practitioners.

The book is structured into different chapters to ensure a systematic examination. Initially, it outlines the relevance of SEO in today's digital landscape. Subsequently, an exploration of the key components of SEO, including off-page and on-page optimization, technical SEO, and local SEO, is conducted. Each section will delve into the strategies involved and best practices to implement, thus giving readers insights they can apply.

To provide practical knowledge and contextual understanding, the book also showcases various case studies highlighting businesses that have successfully implemented SEO strategies and the results they achieved. A chapter is specifically dedicated to unraveling the algorithmic logic of prominent search engines, primarily Google, to give readers an insightful perspective on the workings of these complex systems.

In addition, the book also highlights SEO's potential challenges: ensuring constant website optimization to align with ever-changing search engine algorithms, avoiding penalties from white hat SEO violations, and staying current with the latest SEO trends. Ethical SEO practices that abide by the guidelines set by search engines are emphasized to encourage responsible and effective use of SEO.

The book concludes with a glance at the future of SEO, focusing on mobile optimization, voice search, AI, and other anticipated trends. This final section serves as a guide for readers to continuously adapt their SEO strategies to the evolving digital marketing landscape.

In conclusion, "SEO: A Comprehensive Guide" aims to function as an extensive resource for readers eager to harness the immense potential of SEO. By providing a holistic understanding of SEO and its many facets, the book aims to guide businesses towards digital success in an increasingly online world.

CHAPTER 1 - THE BASICS OF SEO

Definition of SEO

Search Engine Optimization, abbreviated as SEO, is a complex digital marketing strategy that includes numerous techniques, tactics, and best practices dedicated to improving the visibility of a website in search engines (Crestodina, 2020). It is an essential tactic that companies, bloggers, and web developers exploit to draw users to their online platforms without paying for advertisements.

Quite simply, SEO is the process of making alterations to your website design and content to make it more attractive to a search engine. It is a way for the search engine to project your website as the best result among thousands of others that exist on the web bearing the same keywords or phrases (Fishkin, 2018). Every website owner aims to draw more traffic to their site, and the most effective way to do this is to optimize the site for the search engine, allowing the platform to be discovered by more user's who are searching for information that fits precisely what your website has to offer.

The primary function of a search engine is to present users with the most accurate and high-quality results that fulfil their needs. This involves going through thousands of websites to understand what they contain and how valuable their content could be to users (Kiss, 2013). The search engine then ranks the websites based on numerous factors, which are collectively known as the search engine algorithm.

While the exact algorithm used by search engines like Google is mostly a secret, many SEO professionals agree that it includes relevance, quality, usability, and the authority of content. Thus, SEO primarily involves optimizing a website's content and design to meet these expectations, which would help the website rank higher in search results and thus, attract more visitors (Patel, 2020).

It's also important to note that effective SEO practices are not just about pleasing search engines. They are also about pleasing users. Quality content, website usability, and mobile optimization are elements we associate with a good user experience and are as valuable for SEO as they are for user engagement (Turner, 2017).

Moreover, SEO is not just a one-time process but a continuous one. As the algorithms of search engines are always evolving, it's crucial to keep up with these changes to maintain or improve your search rankings. This calls for constant monitoring, testing, and tuning of your SEO strategy.

In a nutshell, SEO is a critical digital marketing strategy that helps increase the visibility of a website in search engine results, making it easier for users to find and engage with your content.

The Function of SEO

Search Engine Optimization (SEO) is a pivotal aspect of digital marketing. It refers to the process of enhancing a website or online content to increase its visibility for relevant searches (Mangools, 2021). The principle behind SEO is straightforward: the higher the visibility of your pages in search engine results, the higher the probability of attracting potential and existing customers to your business platform (Chaffey & Ellis-Chadwick, 2019).

SEO, essentially, serves two main functions. Firstly, it helps improve the visibility and credibility of a business online. This is achieved by optimizing the website or online content with keywords that potential customers use in their search engine queries. Incorporating these keywords improves the chances of the website appearing in the top search results (Patel, 2016).

Secondly, SEO also improves user experience and usability of a website. A well-optimized site that adheres to SEO best practices is likely to have a user-friendly interface, easy navigation, and relevant content. This significantly increases user satisfaction, ultimately contributing to a higher user conversion rate (Chaffey & Ellis-Chadwick, 2019).

These functions of SEO underscore its importance in driving traffic to a website, thus increasing its online presence. By enhancing website visibility and credibility, SEO can influence consumers' perceptions about a brand. This, in turn, can significantly contribute to building brand equity and fostering customer loyalty (Patel, 2016).

The implication for businesses is clear: SEO is not an optional component of digital marketing—it is a necessity. With the internet evolving into the primary platform for commerce and communication, SEO is becoming increasingly crucial for businesses striving to maintain competitive advantage in the digital marketplace (Mangools, 2021).

Even so, SEO is not a one-time task, but a continuous process, which requires on-going adjustments and improvements. Search engine algorithms are updated frequently, making it necessary for businesses to adapt their SEO strategies accordingly (Chaffey & Ellis-Chadwick, 2019).

In conclusion, SEO plays a vital role in enhancing online visibility and credibility, improving user experience, and driving traffic to a business's website. Its strategic implementation ensures the success of a business's digital marketing efforts and, ultimately, its performance in the digital marketplace.

SEO Vs. SEM

Online businesses and brands have become aware of the significance of search engines in the evolution of e-commerce. Typically, the success of a digital marketing strategy lies in a brand's online visibility and exposure. Two prime mechanisms that guarantee such visibility and exposure are Search Engine Optimization (SEO) and Search Engine Marketing (SEM). Although SEO and SEM aim to enhance the presence of a business online, their workings are unique and serve different purposes based on the business's needs and goals (Auer, Furrer, & Surya, 2019).

Search Engine Optimization, or SEO, is the process of increasing website traffic through unpaid or 'organic' search results. This method revolves around incorporating relevant keywords, enhancing website design, and creating high-quality content that attracts and retains users. It involves optimizing individual web pages to rank higher and gain more relevant traffic in search engines. SEO is essentially a long-term strategy that seeks to establish and maintain a notable online presence. A well-optimized website can gain credibility and authority over time, attracting more users organically (Zhang et al., 2018).

Conversely, Search Engine Marketing, or SEM, is the utilization of digital marketing strategies to increase visibility on search engine results pages (SERPs). SEM primarily refers to paid search activities. It involves the promotion of websites by increasing their visibility in SERP's predominantly through paid advertising. SEM offers quick results and is most beneficial for businesses looking to gain immediate visibility and exposure, as they only pay for impressions that result in visitors (Cho & Cheon, 2019).

Although similar in some aspects, the main difference between SEO and SEM lies in how traffic is obtained. SEO focuses on organic traffic, while SEM relies on paid traffic. Therefore, in deciding which strategy to use, one must consider the impact and purpose of the business's digital marketing plan (McGee, 2019). SEO is more suitable for businesses that have time to wait for results and cultivate a strong online brand. But for brands looking for quick high-visibility tactics, SEM is the preferable choice.

Ultimately, both SEO and SEM are crucial aspects of any successful digital marketing strategy. Understanding the advantages and disadvantages of each strategy can help determine how they can effectively serve specific business goals. Therefore, it is advisable for online businesses to incorporate both SEO and SEM strategies for the maximization of their online visibility and reach.

Components of SEO

Search Engine Optimization, commonly referred to as SEO, is a strategic approach to enhancing a website's visibility in search engine results. This drives organic, unpaid traffic to the website, enhancing its credibility and extending its outreach. There are, however, several components of SEO that are key to crafting an effective SEO strategy (Theocharis, 2021).

1. Keyword Research:

Keyword research is one of the most critical components. This involves identifying words and phrases that potential website visitors might input into search engines. Proper keyword research enables you to optimize the SEO in line with the actual search terms people are using, thus funneling your target audience towards your website (Patel, 2021).

2. Content Creation:

The quality and relevancy of your content directly impact your SEO. Good content that is consistently updated will attract more traffic and induce website visitors to stay longer on your webpage. It should ideally be designed around your targeted keywords and offer valuable information that the audience seeks.

3. On-Page Optimization:

On-page optimization refers to actions taken directly within your website to improve its search rankings. This includes optimizing titles, heading, content, and the overall structure. It also includes the use of meta-descriptions and tags, which are brief descriptions of your page's content that appear under your website link on search engine result pages (Enge et al., 2020).

4. Off-Page Optimization:

This involves building backlinks from other websites to complement your on-page optimization. It can help improve the website's reputation and popularity. Because these websites link back to your webpage, it effectively encourages more organic traffic to your site while also improving your standing on search engine result pages.

5. User Experience:

Google has highlighted the importance of putting users first. They enhance their search engine algorithms to ensure that sites offering a great user experience rank higher. This involves ensuring your website is responsive, easy to navigate, and fast to load.

6. Performance Monitoring:

Regular audits and performance monitoring are key to maintain effective SEO. This involves assessing how well your website is performing in search engine rankings and whether your organic traffic is increasing (Enge et al., 2020). It's also important to regularly analyze your strategy and refine it based on these assessments.

Understanding these components will render the process of crafting an effective SEO strategy far more feasible. By taking advantage of these components, businesses can strategically enhance their online presence, drive more organic traffic to their website, and thereby increase their overall outreach and credibility.

Purpose of SEO in Digital Marketing Strategy

Search Engine Optimization (SEO) is a critical component of every digital marketing strategy. The primary purpose of SEO in digital marketing is to improve the visibility and ranking of a website on search engine results pages (SERPs), thereby driving a targeted audience to the website (Patel, 2020).

The digital marketplace is becoming increasingly competitive. Consequently, businesses need to make effective use of SEO to stand out from the competition. SEO improves the organic ranking of a website on SERPs. Organic ranking refers to a website's ranking on a SERP that cannot be influenced by paid advertising. The significance of such ranking cannot be understated as research has shown that websites on the first page of Google garner nearly 95% of web traffic, while subsequent pages receive 5% or less (Chaffey, 2019).

High visibility on SERPs increases the likelihood of potential customers discovering and visiting the business' website. Therefore, SEO plays a vital role in enhancing brand awareness among consumers.

Additionally, SEO is instrumental in achieving targeted marketing, one of the primary goals in digital marketing (Kumar and Rajan, 2020). Targeted marketing involves reaching consumers based on their particular needs, wants, and preferences. SEO involves the use of relevant keywords in website content that potential consumers are likely to use when searching for products or services online. Consequently, an effective SEO strategy ensures that a website appears in the search results of users who are seeking the type of products or services the business offers, thus maximizing the probability of driving quality, targeted traffic to the site.

Moreover, SEO offers longevity in terms of digital presence. While social media trends can wane, and Pay-Per-Click (PPC) campaigns can exhaust a budget, SEO's sustained efforts can offer steady traffic over time (Orth, 2020). For brands seeking a durable online visibility, SEO should be an integral component of their digital marketing strategy.

In conclusion, SEO is not merely a digital marketing tool; it is a critical component that influences the overall success of a digital marketing strategy. Its strategic importance lies in its ability to improve a website's visibility, boost brand awareness, achieve targeted marketing, and provide longevity in digital presence. Hence, businesses seeking to solidify their online presence and reach their target audience effectively must make SEO a cornerstone of their digital marketing strategy.

CHAPTER 2 - SEARCH ENGINES AND ALGORITHMS

Understanding Search Engines (Google, Bing, Yahoo)
Search engines, the best known of which are Google, Bing, and Yahoo, are essential tools in today's digital age. They crawl, index, and rank websites to provide convenient retrieval of information from the massive World Wide Web.

The two fundamental operations that search engines perform are crawling and indexing (Boutell, 2020). Crawling involves search engine robots, also known as spiders or bots, scanning websites for content. These are smart algorithms that visit web pages and follow links on those pages, forming an interconnected web of sorts - not unlike a spider's web. During this procedure, they capture and store data in a data center, which is referred to as indexing. This indexed information forms the backbone of search engine results. When you enter a search query, the engine looks up the index and presents the most relevant websites based on a variety of ranking factors.

Google, Bing, and Yahoo have unique indexing algorithms. Google, dominating with a staggering 92.47% market share in 2021 (Statcounter, 2021), is known for its highly complex and proprietary algorithm. It takes over 200 factors into consideration, including website relevance, user experience, site speed, and mobile-friendliness.

Bing, owned by Microsoft, has a market share of about 2.69% (Statcounter, 2021). Although Bing's indexing algorithm is not made public, digital marketing specialists believe it focuses on the relevance of social media integration and technical SEO factors like page load speed and keyword density.

Yahoo, once a powerful search engine, has significantly fallen behind with only 1.47% market share (Statcounter, 2021). Yahoo now uses Bing's technology for its search engine operations. It is essential to note that despite differences in algorithms, all search engines prioritize relevance, quality of content, and the user experience in their ranking.

SEO (Search Engine Optimization) is a strategy commonly used by website owners to rank higher in search engine results. SEO techniques primarily focus on creating quality content, optimizing website design, and building reputable links. Being familiar with the working principles of search engines can significantly improve the effectiveness of SEO strategies.

In conclusion, search engines like Google, Bing, and Yahoo provide a unique gateway to the immense wealth of information on the internet. By understanding their working mechanisms, businesses and web enthusiasts can better leverage these tools for information retrieval and website visibility, thus optimizing their online presence.

Search Engine Algorithms

In the rapidly evolving world of information technology, Search Engine Algorithms play an instrumental role in efficiently connecting users with the desired content from an enormous data pool. To understand this system better, it is fundamental to unearth the intricate structure of such algorithms that powers our daily internet usage (Beel, et.al., 2010).

Explanation of Algorithms

What makes a website appear on the first page of Google results is a question perhaps all internet users posed at least once. The answer lies in an intricate choreography of algorithms that are part and parcel of Search Engine Optimization (SEO). SEO algorithms are the mathematical instructions that determine a website's ranking on search engines like Google, Bing, or Yahoo (Napierkowski, 2021).

SEO works by communicating to search engines about a website's relevance and usefulness to particular queries, thereby enhancing its visibility. To decipher the value and relevance of a website, search engines employ different algorithms (Orchard, 2019). The precise composition of these algorithms remains a closely guarded secret, though some of their key components can be understood and optimized for improved SEO performance.

To begin with, one of the critical facets of these algorithms is related to the keywords used in a website's content. Keywords are phrases that potential site visitors might use during a search. Search engine algorithms index these keywords and prioritize web pages where they appear prominently and meaningfully (Napierkowski, 2021).

Secondly, search engines consider the quality of a website's content. If a webpage provides insightful, accurate, and well-crafted information, it is likely to rank higher. Unique and regularly updated content also signals to search engines that a website is active and valuable (Chaffey & Ellis-Chadwick, 2019).

Another critical attribute is the number and quality of links, both inbound and outbound, associated with a website. If a site is referenced by reliable and high-ranking websites, algorithms interpret it as a credible source, hence improving its ranking (Patel, 2016).

Additionally, search engine algorithms account for a website's user experience. Factors like the website's load speed, mobile-friendliness, secure connection (HTTPS), and smooth navigation all contribute to a positive user experience, which is favorably acknowledged by search engine algorithms (Ledford, 2020).

Furthermore, the algorithms factor in the social signals of a website, such as likes, shares, and comments on social media platforms (Patel, 2016). The greater the website's interaction level on social media, the higher its chances of appearing more prominently in search results.

In conclusion, understanding how the SEO algorithms operate can greatly enhance website visibility and ranking. By incorporating suitable keywords, generating high-quality content, accumulating robust links, improving user experience, and boosting social signals, any website can increase its SEO performance and make its mark in the sea of digital content.

Search Engine Algorithms, at their core, are complex computer programs that facilitate the search function by crawling, indexing, and ranking digital content. The intent is to present search results that primarily match users' inquiries (Broder, 2002).

The process starts with crawling, where search engines deploy web spiders or crawlers to find content across the internet. They follow links within and across platforms, identifying new and updated content in websites, blog posts, digital images, or videos.

Next, the discovered content is organized into an index, much like a vast library catalog. All data collected by the crawlers are compiled and stored in this index, including key signals from the websites like keywords, site freshness, and more.

Lastly, the ranking process involves the algorithm parsing the index to deliver the most relevant search results to users based on their specific queries. Each search engine uses different, often proprietary, algorithms to rank indexed content (Amsler, 2018).

Apart from the primary factors like relevance and quality, these algorithms consider numerous other criteria in their ranking protocols. Some such factors include the reliability and authority of linked websites, the content's perceived usefulness according to user behavior data, the device and location of the user, page loading speeds, and mobile-friendliness, among many others (Gao & Liu, 2008).

As a result, search engine optimization (SEO) has become a critical tool for businesses striving for digital visibility. It involves optimizing web pages to align with these algorithmic demands to appear at the top of search results, thereby increasing website traffic (Chung, 2017).

However, it is crucial to understand that such algorithms are not static. Companies periodically revise them, maintaining a dynamic response to user needs, changing technologies, and potential exploitations. Notably, Google, the leading search engine, reportedly updates its algorithm approximately 500-600 times annually (Fishkin, 2017).

In conclusion, search engine algorithms consistently strive for an optimum user experience by delivering relevant and high-quality result sets. Because of their highly dynamic nature and complex structure, understanding these algorithms is a necessary step towards developing effective SEO strategies.

Factors Influencing Algorithms

Search Engine Optimization (SEO) has become all-important in today's era of digital marketing. It plays a pivotal role in expanding the online visibility of websites, and thereby augments the prospects of businesses. The central players in this realm of SEO are the search engine algorithms which govern the way search engine results are produced. It is essential to comprehend these algorithms and their influential SEO factors for to effectively strategize digital marketing campaigns (Chaffey, 2021).

One of the significant SEO factors that influence search engine algorithms is the quality content. Content is the backbone of any SEO strategy as search engines strive to provide their users with the most relevant and high-quality results. Good quality and fresh content, enriched with proper keywords and information, help improve a website's SEO ranking (Patel, 2019).

Keyword optimization is another crucial factor. Search engines use keyword matching to bridge the gap between user queries and suitable websites. The right keywords, coupled with optimum keyword density, can improve the search engine's perception of a webpage's relevancy to a specific query.

User experience (UX) is also a substantial factor that algorithms consider. Increases in dwell time and page views indirectly signify that users find the page content valuable. Consequently, good UX is likely to improve SEO performance. According to Google, User Experience is directly related to page experience and is considered one of the ranking factors (Google, 2020).

Backlinks - links pointing to your site from others - are another contributor to SEO rankings. Backlinks from high-authority websites are a merit sign for search engines. They consider these as votes of confidence, demonstrating that the linked site has worthwhile content, thus promoting it higher in search rankings.

Social signals are also being increasingly recognized as a contributing factor. When content from a site is widely shared on social platforms, search algorithms interpret this as a sign of quality content, which can positively influence SEO ranking (Chaffey, 2021).

Importantly, mobile-optimization has grown in relevance with the increase in smartphone usage. Since Google introduced its mobile-first indexing, mobile-friendly sites are favored in mobile search results, making this a crucial aspect of SEO (Google, 2018).

In conclusion, multiple interrelated factors contribute to search engine rankings. Understanding these factors and the way they affect search engine algorithms can help businesses create a robust SEO plan. Furthermore, keeping up with current SEO trends and algorithm updates will ensure that a website stays relevant, accessible, and competitive in the rapidly evolving digital marketplace.

The Impact of Algorithm Changes on SEO

In the digital era, maintaining an online presence is crucial. Search Engine Optimization (SEO) has become essential for businesses to rank higher in search results, attract more traffic, and enhance online visibility. However, given the dynamic nature of search engine algorithms, businesses and SEO professionals must adapt to changes to maintain or improve their rankings.

Search engine algorithms are computer programs that determine the rankings of web pages in search results. They analyze different factors and decide the order of the pages that appear for any given keyword search. Some of these factors include site quality, keyword relevance, user experience, and backlinks among others (Search Engine Journal, 2019).

Several major search engines, such as Google, continually tweak their ranking algorithms to improve the relevancy and quality of their search results. This continuous modification of search engine algorithms significantly impacts SEO strategies.

When search engines update their algorithms, they can shake up the rankings dramatically. Sites previously enjoying top positions may slide down, whereas those occupying lower positions may ascend. For example, Google's Panda update in 2011 affected approximately 12% of all search results, punishing sites with low-quality content and rewarding those with high-quality, unique content (Moz, 2012).

Search engine algorithm updates necessitate changes in SEO strategies. For instance, Google's Penguin update in 2012 targeted websites heavily relying on over-optimized anchor texts and those participating in link schemes. After the update, these previously effective tactics became risky, compelling SEO professionals to prioritize natural link building and proper keyword usage (Moz, 2013).

Moreover, recent algorithm changes aiming to provide better responses to voice search queries have led SEO professionals to adopt conversational keyword phrases and aim for featured snippets, radically transforming conventional SEO techniques (SEMrush, 2018).

Conclusively, staying abreast of the major algorithm changes is crucial in the SEO world. While these changes can pose significant challenges, they also present opportunities for businesses and websites to focus on making their content not just to rank higher but also useful and meaningful for users. Positioning the user at the center of SEO strategies can ultimately lead to better rankings and website traffic, regardless of algorithm updates.

Introduction to SERPs

SERPs, also known as Search Engine Results Pages, are web pages delivered to users when they search for something online using a search engine, such as Google or Bing. In essence, SERPs are the web search engine's response to a user's search query (1).

For every search query, search engine algorithms evaluate millions of pages to provide an ordered list of results that best match the search query and are most relevant to the user's request. This process is accomplished with complex algorithms that take into account numerous factors, such as the quality of the content on the page, the relevance to the search query, the authority of the website, and the user experience (2).

The main component of SERPs is the listing of results returned by the search engine in response to a keyword query; however, they can include other types of content, such as advertisements, images, news chapters, maps, and knowledge panels. The results are usually positioned in decreasing order of relevance, with the most relevant results appearing at the top of the SERPs (3).

There are two types of results on SERPs: organic results and paid results. Organic results are listings that match the user's query based on relevance. These are not paid advertisements and cannot be bought. Ad algorithms determine them—you cannot pay for higher organic search rankings. On the other hand, paid results are advertisements that appear at the top or side of SERPs (4). Organic search results are crucial for website visibility because they attract the majority of user clicks. Various SEO techniques help improve a website's search rankings, including keyword optimization, link building, and creating high-quality content that appeals to users. Conversely, paid results are crucial for businesses looking to gain immediate visibility for specific keywords (5).

Understanding SERPs is vital for marketers, SEO professionals, and website owners. With the right SEO strategy, a website can move up in SERPs, garner more online visibility, and attract more potential customers (6).

In conclusion, SERPs are an essential component of the online search experience, shaping user interaction with the web. They are the gateway between users and the content they seek, providing ordered lists of relevant results based on complex ranking algorithms. By understanding and optimizing for SERPs, businesses can significantly enhance their online visibility and digital marketing efforts.

CHAPTER 3 - KEYWORDS FUNDAMENTALS IN SEO

Role and Importance of Keywords

In the ever-evolving world of digital marketing and search engine optimization, keywords play a quintessential role. They serve as the foundation for all your online marketing efforts, driving traffic to your website and making your content discoverable to the vast Internet audience. This chapter will explore the significance and use of keywords in enhancing online visibility and marketing strategy.

The function of keywords primarily lies in their use for search engine optimization (SEO). They are words or phrases that potential clients type into search engines like Google when looking for specific products or services. By effectively incorporating these terms into your web content, you dramatically enhance your chances of appearing in search results related to your business(1).

For instance, a home improvement store might use keywords such as "DIY projects," "home décor ideas," or "affordable furniture," aiming to capture the attention of consumers searching for these topics online. This practice helps attract more site visitors who could then be converted into customers.

Furthermore, keywords help define your brand and its offerings. They depict what you do, the products or services you offer, and what sets you apart from your competition (2). This understanding makes it simpler for potential customers to recognize and select your company amidst a sea of online options.

Additionally, keyword usage aids in creating targeted marketing campaigns. By employing the correct keywords, you guarantee that your content reaches the right audience – people who are genuinely interested in what you have to offer. This strategy results in more efficient use of marketing resources, translating into increased return-on-investment (ROI) (3).

However, it is vital to mention that keyword implementation in digital marketing requires careful planning and strategy. Keyword stuffing, or overuse of keywords, can lead to penalties from search engines. Essentially, your keywords should flow naturally within your content and should always maintain relevancy to the topic (4).

In conclusion, keywords are integral to digital marketing. They aid in enhancing online visibility, defining the brand, creating targeted marketing campaigns and eventually increasing ROI. To effectively leverage the power of keywords, it is pivotal to utilize them appropriately, avoiding practices like keyword stuffing that can negatively impact your website's SEO.

As the world of digital marketing continues to evolve, the prominence of keywords remains undeniable. Understand your audience, research your keywords, and integrate them into your content to enjoy their many benefits.

How to Conduct Keyword Research

Keyword research is an integral part of any successful SEO strategy. At the heart of every Search Engine Optimization campaign lies a dire need to understand how your potential customers search for products, services or information relevant to your industry. This chapter will guide you through the process of conducting effective keyword research.

Firstly, to conduct comprehensive keyword research, you need a good keyword research tool. Google's Keyword Planner is among the best free tools available (1). It provides vital data like average monthly searches, competition level, and estimated bid cost of keywords. Also, there are paid keyword research tools like SEMRush, Ahrefs and Moz that offers more advanced features.

Identifying relevant topics pertinent to your business is the initial step of keyword research. This involves breaking down the broader business category into smaller, more manageable topic buckets. For instance, if you deal with digital marketing, your broader topics could include social media marketing, content marketing, and email marketing.

The next important step is to find keywords related to these topics. Use your keyword research tool to generate a list of keyword ideas. Type in the broad topics, and the tool would provide relevant keyword suggestions. The aim is to identify both head keywords and long-tail keywords. Head keywords are usually short and generic, often consisting of one or two words with high search volumes. Long-tail keywords, however, are more specific, usually comprising three or more words (2).

Closely related to this is the process of understanding the searcher's intent. While some users might be looking for general information (informational intent), others might want to make a purchase (transactional intent). Combining both types in your keyword strategy helps to attract different types of users at different stages of the customer journey.

The final part of the keyword research process is to analyze the competition. This is about finding out who your competitors are and what keywords they rank for. Tools like SEMRush and Ahrefs are excellent for competitor analysis, providing insights into the complexity of ranking for certain keywords.

In conclusion, keyword research isn't just about finding high volume terms to rank for; it's more about finding the right keywords that your potential customers are using. By knowing and understanding these "suitable" keywords, you can create content that your target audience wants to see and increase traffic to your website.

Tools to Simplify Keyword Search

Search Engine Optimization (SEO) is an indispensable part of digital marketing that targets visibility in organic search engine results. A key element of SEO is Keyword search, a technique that involves identifying certain words or phrases relevant to a website's content. These keywords help search engines associate content with search queries, making the content more discoverable and resulting in an increase in traffic. However, identifying the right keywords is not always straightforward. Thankfully, several tools are available that can help simplify this process.

The most recognizable tool in this domain is Google Keyword Planner. This tool is particularly useful as it enables users to discover new keywords related to their business, estimate the search volume of these keywords, and understand how keyword performance changes over time. With adjustable settings for location, language, and search network, the Google Keyword Planner allows for more targeted and effective keyword search (Google Ads, n.d.).

Another important tool in keyword search is Keywords Everywhere. This browser add-on shows keyword data directly on web browsers, making keyword information instantly accessible to users. It provides the monthly search volume, cost per click, and competition data for keywords on multiple websites. These statistics can guide users when choosing the best keywords for their content (Keywords Everywhere, n.d.).

SEMrush is a popular SEO tool that includes a comprehensive keyword research feature. With this tool, users can find the right keywords based on factors such as keyword difficulty, number of search results, trend, and search volume. SEMrush can also offer related keywords, phrase matches, and long-tail keywords, widening the scope of potential keywords users can employ (SEMrush, n.d.).

Long Tail Pro is a tool designed to help users locate long-tail keywords. These keywords are more specific and less common, meaning they have less competition and can be beneficial for niche markets. Long Tail Pro also includes a competitive analysis feature, helping users understand the competition they will face when using different keywords (Long Tail Pro, n.d.).

Ahrefs, a tool well-known for backlinks analysis, also has a robust keyword explorer feature. It provides keyword ideas from a database of over 7 billion keywords, updated monthly. It also reveals annual search volume trends, keyword difficulty, and click metrics for top-ranking pages (Ahrefs, n.d.).

In conclusion, keyword search plays a crucial role in SEO, and using the right tools can greatly simplify the process. The tools mentioned above, including Google Keyword Planner, Keywords Everywhere, SEMrush, Long Tail Pro, and Ahrefs, provide useful resources that enable users to conduct effective keyword searches that can help drive traffic to their websites.

Understanding Long Tail Keywords

In the era of digital marketing and e-commerce, the application of Search Engine Optimization (SEO) techniques is crucial in achieving online visibility and attracting website traffic. One such SEO technique that is gaining traction among marketing professionals is the use of long tail keywords. This technique focuses on saturating web content, whether in text or tags, with specific phrases known as keywords, that are likely to be used by online users when conducting internet searches. Understanding the use and benefits of long tail keywords can significantly enhance your SEO strategy.

Long tail keywords are multi-word phrases, typically three or more, which are unique and specific to your product or service. These are much less competitive than generic one or two-word keywords because they attract less overall search volume (Patel, 2020). However, even though long tail keywords cater to fewer searches, they characteristically bring in more targeted traffic and lead to higher conversion rates.

With an understanding of long tail keywords, it becomes easier to generate high-quality content that satisfies users' specific queries. For instance, a user searching for "women's red leather boots size 6" is likely further along in the buying cycle than someone who merely searches "boots". Therefore, if your website content utilizes this long tail keyword, the chances of that individual becoming a customer are significantly higher.

Marketers are leveraging long tail keywords in their SEO strategy because these specific phrases align well with the voice search feature, a rising trend in online searches. With the upsurge of Siri, Alexa, and Google Assistant, users are adapting natural language tone and lengthier, more detailed search phrases which often translate to long tail keywords (Lee, 2019).

Another benefit of using long tail keywords involves the website's ranking on search engine results. The specificity of long tail keywords implies less competition, thus increasing the chances of ranking higher on search engine result pages (SERPs). Even though long tail keywords attract less traffic overall, the increased relevance to the user's search query can improve click-through-rates and overall website rankings.

However, it is essential to ensure the long tail keywords used are relevant to your product or service and regularly used by the targeted audience. SEMrush, Google Keyword Planner, and Ahrefs are a few helpful tools for keyword research (Voorvart, 2018). Using these tools, you can analyze the popularity of specific keywords, their competition levels, and estimate potential traffic.

In conclusion, long tail keywords are an essential part of an effective SEO strategy, offering a more targeted approach to user queries. By understanding and effectively employing these phrases, businesses can improve their online visibility, improve conversion rates, and reshape their digital marketing strategy.

Keyword Optimization and Placement

With the rapid advancements in digital marketing, the importance of keyword optimization and placement has escalated for businesses seeking to enhance their online visibility. Focusing on keyword optimization is fundamental because it significantly influences how search engines comprehend and index your web content, which, in turn, determines your website's ranking in search engine results pages (SERPs) (Patel, 2020). Successfully executed, keyword optimization can lead to improved online visibility, more organic traffic, higher conversion rates, and increased brand awareness.

Keyword optimization revolves around carefully researching, analyzing, selecting, and employing the right keywords in your content to align with what searchers are looking for (Fishkin, 2012). The ultimate intent is to discern and effectively satisfy the search intent of your target audience. This process, when appropriately executed, establishes a transparent, conversational pathway between you and prospective consumers.

On the other hand, keyword placement refers to the strategic positioning of keywords throughout your content such that it improves search engine rankings. Key locations for keyword placement include the title tag, meta description, URL, headings (H1, H2, etc.), image alt text, and, naturally, within the content body (Patel, 2020). It's important to note that while placing keywords throughout your content, moderation is key to avoid keyword stuffing—an offense viewed negatively by Google and other search engines.

The significance of keyword optimization and placement, however, goes beyond gaining a high SERP ranking. These tactics help communicate the purpose of your content to visitors, thus enhancing user experience (UX). A well-optimized website facilitates users to find the information they need more rapidly and accurately, making your site more user-friendly (Fishkin, 2012).

Despite the numerous benefits, there are challenges. One of the most prevalent is keyword cannibalization, where multiple pages on the same website compete for the same keywords. This dilutes the relevance and authority of your pages, negatively impacting your SERP rankings (Patel, 2019).

In conclusion, keyword optimization and placement remain crucial for successfully navigating the digital marketing landscape. They are essential components of SEO and contribute significantly to improving online visibility, organic traffic, user experience, and overall brand reputation.

CHAPTER 4 - CONTENT MARKETING AND SEO

Importance of Quality Content in SEO

In optimizing a website for search engines, implementing the most effective SEO (Search Engine Optimization) strategies is undoubtedly essential. However, in the midst of technical considerations, the importance of quality content often gets overlooked. As Google steadily enhances its algorithms, high-quality, relevant, and engaging content has emerged as a critical element in driving website traffic, improving search engine rankings, and gaining a competitive edge in the digital sphere (Stan Ventures, 2021).

To fully grasp the significance of quality content in SEO, it is necessary to understand Google's central principle – delivering a superior user experience. Google's main goal is to deliver the most relevant, valuable, and comprehensive content to users based on their search queries. Berkley (2020) even posits that "content is king" in the world of SEO. Websites that offer excellent content are more likely to be suggested to users by Google, which in turn improves the sites' SEO ranking.

The quality of the content is a key determinant of a webpage's relevance. A well-written chapter that effectively serves the needs of the users is considered high-quality content. It should provide clear and accurate information, answer common queries or solve problems, and be organized and formatted in a user-friendly manner. Poorly crafted content, irrespective of the intensity of SEO techniques applied, will struggle to retain the user's attention and consequently, its SEO ranking will suffer (Marwick, 2021).

The engagement level of the content also holds immense significance in SEO. Engaging content is liked, commented upon, and shared more frequently - all of which signal to search engines that the content is valuable and relevant, hence pushing up its ranking. Furthermore, unique and engaging content boosts organic traffic – each share, for instance, can bring in a new reader who could potentially become a return visitor (HubSpot, 2018).

Another notable aspect is the role quality content plays in link building, an integral part of SEO. High-quality, original content naturally attracts backlinks from other sites, thereby enhancing the website's credibility and possibly its ranking on Google (Marie Haynes Consulting, 2019).

In conclusion, quality content is crucial for SEO because it aligns with Google's principle of providing a superior user experience. It determines webpage relevance, enhances engagement, and supports link building. Thus, it's imperative that webmasters and SEO strategists prioritize the creation and delivery of quality content, which is as crucial, if not more, as other technical aspects of SEO.

Guidelines for Creating SEO-Friendly Content

In the landscape of digital marketing, Search Engine Optimization (SEO) occupies a position of paramount significance. Ranking high on Google and related search engines not only channels organic traffic to your website but also cements your reputation among various stakeholders. However, a dominant challenge in capitalizing on SEO is the creation of SEO-friendly content. This difficulty arises due to the constant evolution of search engine algorithms, which demand correspondingly flexible and adaptive content strategies. This chapter will discuss guidelines for creating SEO-friendly content.

The foundation of SEO-friendly content is keyword research. Strategic and appropriate use of keywords ensures your content remains compatible with search engines' algorithms and user search patterns. Tools like Google Keyword Planner, SEMrush and Moz Keyword Explorer can facilitate effective keyword planning (1). It is also crucial to include long-tail keywords as they often devise the optimal strategies for reaching niche audiences and driving conversions.

Optimizing your content's title and metadata is another fundamental step. An impactful headline, incisive SEO title, and a compelling meta description can significantly enhance the visibility of your content on search engines. Use your primary keyword in both the SEO title and meta description while ensuring that they are within the recommended character limit set by search engines.

Structured content, with proper use of H1, H2, and H3 headings, is easier for search engine bots to understand and index. It also ensures that your content is readable and engaging to the user. Subheadings can use secondary and related keywords, providing further depth to your SEO efforts.

In a similar vein, the readability of your content is pivotal for SEO ranking. Search engines favor easy-to-understand content that provides value to the user. The Flesch-Kincaid readability tests can be a useful benchmark for your content's readability.

A salient aspect often overlooked is the optimization of images. Compress your images, use descriptive file names, and ensure each image has an ALT tag containing a relevant keyword.

Lastly, backlinks and internal links enhance the credibility of your content and influence search engine rankings positively. High-quality backlinks from reputable sites signal to search engines that your content is reliable and valuable. Internal linking not only enhances the user experience by providing them with additional relevant content but also helps search engine bots navigate your site efficiently.

In sum, the journey of creating SEO-friendly content involves a delicate dance amongst multiple elements. A keen understanding of evolving algorithms, the intelligent use of keywords, careful metadata creation, and quality backlinks are fundamental. Simultaneously, engaging, structured, and readable content can significantly influence your SEO rankings.

Engagement and Relevance in SEO Content

Approximately 93% of online experiences kick off with a search engine (Imforza, 2021) which has significantly enhanced the importance of Search Engine Optimization (SEO) in digital marketing strategies. One of the most crucial components of SEO involves the development of high-quality, engaging, and relevant content. Hence, this chapter aims to delve into the importance of engagement and relevance in SEO content.

Engagement in SEO content refers to an individual's interaction level with your website content. High engagement indicates that users find value in your content, encouraging them to spend more time on your site. It could be in either form – reading blogs, watching videos, leaving comments, or sharing posts – all these actions speak volumes about the effectiveness of content in capturing users' interest (TheeDigital, 2021).

SEO and content are versatile digital marketing tools that fundamentally aim to satisfy user intent. In fact, Google's algorithm rewards websites that consistently provide engaging, high-quality content because this is what users are searching for. In essence, engagement contributes to lower bounce rates, higher dwell time and better conversion rates, which ultimately can result in improved SEO rankings (HubSpot, 2021).

Next comes relevance in SEO content. This connotes the significance and usefulness of content to the target audience. This is what answers the user's query, solves their problems, and meets their needs. Irrespective of how frequently you update your website or use keywords, if the content is not relevant to the users, you are less likely to rank higher on search engines (Moz, 2021).

A simple way to enhance relevance is to understand your target audience and their requirements better. This can be achieved through keyword research, analyzing search intent, and using relevant topics. Additionally, consistently updating your content can help maintain its relevance (SearchEngineJournal, 2021).

Achieving a balance between engagement and relevance in SEO content could be a game-changer. Integrating these attributes can lead to better SEO rankings, increased visibility, and improved brand reputation.

In conclusion, for a successful SEO strategy, creating content that offers a mix of engagement and relevance should be a priority. While SEO techniques can bring users to your pages, only valuable, intriguing and timely content can keep them there.

Role of Blogging and Chapter Writing in SEO

Search engine optimization (SEO) continues to be a vital tool within the digital marketing landscape. Among the diverse strategies deployed for SEO, blogging and chapter writing remain central. This chapter evaluates the role that blogging and chapter writing play in SEO.

A 2018 report by SEO Tribunal showed that 70-80% of search engine users focused primarily on organic results, ignoring paid advertisements (1). More importantly, 57% of marketers declared that SEO-generated content, particularly written blog chapters, had brought in the most leads for their companies (2). These findings underscore the importance of having quality written content, but why do blogs and chapters contribute significantly to SEO?

Firstly, blogging and chapter writing boost keyword optimization. By successfully embedding relevant keywords in your blogs and chapters, search engines can identify and rank your website effectively. The higher the ranking, the greater your website's visibility, translating into a higher probability of web traffic and conversion rates (3).

Secondly, blogs and chapters provide fresh content, which is a key ranking factor for search engines. Google, especially, favors regularly updated content, seeing it as a reliable source of information. By continuously updating your blog with chapters, you give search engines fresh content to index, which improves your site's rank (4).

Thirdly, blogs and chapters improve dwell time and user engagement metrics. High-quality blogs and chapters encourage visitors to spend more time on your site to read and interact with the content. Longer dwell times indicate to search engines that your site offers value, which can improve your ranking (5).

Lastly, blogs and chapters lay the foundation for backlinking, an SEO tactic where other websites link back to your site. Providing valuable content increases chances of other sites linking to your site, thus increasing your domain authority. Higher domain authority ultimately has a positive impact on site ranking (6).

In conclusion, the role of chapter writing and blogging in SEO cannot be overstated. They help in keyword optimization, providing fresh content, enhancing user engagement, and encouraging backlinks, leading to improved site ranking. Thus, businesses and individuals hoping to enhance their web presence for maximum visibility cannot ignore the power of blogs and chapters in SEO.

Mobile Optimization for Content

Introduction

Mobile optimization is undeniably one of the critical components of online content creation in today's technology-driven society. As per Statista, there are over 6.4 billion smartphone users worldwide as of 2021, exhibiting a steady growth from previous years (1). Hence, crafting content adaptable for mobile is essential for businesses to maintain relevance and optimize user experience.

Understanding Mobile Optimization

Mobile optimization refers to the process of modifying your website content to ensure it displays correctly and efficiently on mobile devices. It encompasses aspects like redesigning the website layout, modifying menus and navigation systems, and resizing images to fit smaller screens. With Google's transition to mobile-first indexing, mobile optimization is not an option but a necessity for online visibility (2).

Value of Mobile Optimization

Mobile optimization holds the potential to improve the user experience, increase dwell time and lower bounce rates. Websites that are not optimized for mobile can frustrate users, causing them to abandon the website and search elsewhere. This dissatisfaction not only tarnishes your brand image but also negatively impacts your page ranking on search engines.

Moreover, mobile optimization is key to reaching more clients and maintaining competitiveness. Mobile users continue to exceed desktop users, indicating that the majority of your potential clientele is on mobile. According to eMarketer, people spend over 3.5 hours on their mobile devices daily, providing an abundant audience for mobile-optimized content (3).

Implementing Mobile Optimization

For effective mobile optimization, readability is paramount. Utilize larger font sizes, incorporate bullet points, and make use of white space for easy legibility. Quick page loading speeds are equally impactful, as delays can increase bounce rates and harm SEO ranking. Open source tools like Google's Accelerated Mobile Pages (AMP) can help to enhance page loading speed (4).

Another potent technique is to make your website navigation mobile-friendly. Websites should have a responsive design adjusting according to the viewports. Also, it is crucial to ensure that all the features and content available for desktop-users are available for mobile-users - the principle of content parity.

Furthermore, implement local SEO strategies. With the popularity of "near me" searches, localized content allows reaching audiences who are ready to convert, thus improving business performance.

Conclusion

Mobile optimization is a significant element in today's mobile-first world. Companies must prioritize mobile optimization to ensure an exemplary user experience, optimize SEO ranking, and reach wider audiences. Embracing these strategies guarantees increased brand visibility, superior user experience, and ultimately, improved business performance.

CHAPTER 5 - LINK BUILDING AND SEO

The Concept of Link Building

Link building refers to the process of acquiring hyperlinks from other websites to your own. A hyperlink, or simply put, a link, is a way for users to navigate between pages on the internet. Search engines like Google use these links to crawl the web; they will crawl the links between the individual pages on your website, and they will crawl the links between entire websites (Moz, 2020).

Effective link building allows search engines to discover new web pages and determine how a page should rank in their search results. This happens during the process of search engine optimization (SEO). Once search engines have crawled pages on the web, they can extract the content from these pages and add them to their indexes (Search Engine Watch, 2018).

Here, they can decide whether a page is of sufficient quality to be ranked for relevant keywords. When they are deciding this, search engines do not only consider the content of the page but also the number of links pointing to that page from external websites and the quality of those external websites. Generally, the more high-quality websites that link to you, the more likely you are to rank well in search results (Pattabhiram, 2019).

There are several techniques of link building, and while they vary in difficulty, SEO experts agree that link building is one of the hardest parts of their jobs. Some of these techniques include content creation & promotion, submission to directories, reviews/testimonials, and getting links from friends, partners, among others. In order for you to build links, you need to have something of value to build links to. In general, building links is most about creating valuable content and making people aware of it (Ahrefs, 2019).

It's essential to understand that certain link-building tactics may land you into trouble with search engines. The need for real, valuable links has never been higher, and it's crucial to stick to ethical and acceptable link-building strategies. Search engines are continually working towards improving their technology to crawls the web more deeply and return increasingly relevant search results to users (KissMetrics, 2020).

To surmise, link building is a key component of successful SEO strategy. It involves an assortment of techniques designed to boost your website's visibility by linking it to relevant, high-quality websites. However, considering the complexity and demanding nature of link-building, it requires expert management and consistent monitoring to ensure its maximum effectiveness.

Importance of High-Quality Backlinks

The relevance and significance of high-quality backlinks in Search Engine Optimization (SEO) cannot be understated. Essentially, backlinks, also known as inbound links or incoming links, are created when one website provides a link to another. They are vital to SEO as they can have a profound impact on the visibility and ranking of a website on search engine result pages (SERPs). Regarded as votes of confidence from one site to another, high-quality backlinks indicate to search engines that the linked content is valuable, reliable and informative to users (Patel, 2018). This chapter discusses why high-quality backlinks are so essential in SEO.

Firstly, high-quality backlinks can boost the credibility and trustworthiness of a website. In search engine algorithms, the quantity and more importantly, the quality of backlinks a website receives can help establish its authenticity, relevance and authority on the internet. Websites that obtain links from high-authority domains are typically viewed as more dependable and authoritative in their specific industry or niche (Lu, 2020). Thus, investing in high-quality backlinks can significantly enhance your online reputation and standing.

Secondly, high-quality backlinks increase a website's visibility and ranking on SERPs. Google and other popular search engines consider backlinks as a crucial ranking factor in their algorithms. Whenever a website receives a high-quality backlink, search engines interpret this as a positive endorsement of its content, which can subsequently improve its ranking position on SERPs (Google, 2019). An improved ranking not only guarantees more organic traffic but also increases the chances of attracting more high-quality backlinks.

Moreover, high-quality backlinks can lead to faster indexing. Search engine bots discover new webpages by following backlinks from existing webpages. Therefore, having backlinks from high-authority sites can aid in faster discovery and indexing of your webpages by search engines.

Lastly, high-quality backlinks can generate referral traffic, which refers to visitors who land on your website by clicking on a link from another site. As high-quality backlinks are generally obtained from relevant and popular websites, they are likely to attract a significant number of highly targeted, relevant traffic to your site (Moz, 2021).

In conclusion, the importance of high-quality backlinks cannot be overstated. They not only boost the credibility of a website but also improve its visibility and ranking on SERPs, lead to faster indexing, and generate referral traffic. Given these significant benefits, it is prudent for every website owner and digital marketer to prioritize building high-quality backlinks as part of their SEO strategy.

Strategy for Obtaining Valuable Backlinks

Initiating and maintaining a strong online presence is crucial in digital marketing. One effective way to boost your online presence is through obtaining valuable backlinks. These backlinks are an essential component of Search Engine Optimization (SEO) as they function to increase online visibility, enhance web traffic, and establish your site's authority and trustworthiness (Neil Patel, 2016). Therefore, understanding effective strategies for acquiring valuable backlinks is paramount. In this chapter, we'll delve into robust strategies that can help your website garner quality backlinks.

Firstly, content creation remains a potent strategy. Your website should offer high-quality, informative content that other site owners would find valuable enough to link to (Search Engine Journal, 2020). Whether it's in-depth research, educational chapters, or engaging visuals, great content naturally attracts backlinks. Also, regularly updating your content keeps it relevant, thereby increasing its linking potential.

Public Relations (PR) also play a vital role in gaining quality backlinks. Establish good relationships with publishers, influencers, and bloggers related to your industry. This can potentially open doors to guest posting opportunities, interviews, or content collaborations that can result in beneficial backlinks.

Next, consider using your competitors' backlinks to your advantage. Tools like SEMRush or Ahrefs allow you to analyze your competitors' backlink profiles. Look for websites that link to your competitor's site but not yours and reach out to them with quality content they might find worth linking to.

Moreover, broken link building is an underutilized yet effective strategy in obtaining valuable backlinks. Look for broken links on relevant websites, create content that matches the broken content and reach out to site owners, offering your link as a replacement (Moz, 2015).

Lastly, social networking sites are useful platforms for attracting backlinks. By promoting your content on these channels, you may attract the attention of bloggers, journalists, or businesses who may end up linking to your site from their blogs or websites.

While these strategies are bound to assist in obtaining valuable backlinks, it's important to understand that gaining meaningful backlinks is a gradual process. It demands patience, effort, and consistency. Stay focused on creating exceptional, shareable content and building solid relationships within your industry.

In the realm of SEO, backlinks are not just about quantity, but more about quality. The focus should be on obtaining valuable backlinks from reputable sites that align with your brand and industry. These backlinks not only contribute to improving your search rankings but also play a pivotal role in driving referral traffic and amplifying your brand's authority.

Understanding the Disavow Tool

The world of Search Engine Optimization (SEO) is complex and continuously evolving. One crucial tool that any website owner or SEO expert should have in their arsenal is the Disavow Tool. This tool, made available by Google, plays an essential role in maintaining the health and effectiveness of your website's backlink profile. This chapter seeks to demystify the Disavow Tool, elucidating its functionality and importance in the realm of SEO.

The Disavow Tool is primarily used to tell Google's algorithm to discount certain backlinks when assessing a website's ranking. These links are typically "bad" or "unnatural" in nature – essentially, ones that could negatively impact the website's SEO (Qode Interactive, 2019).

This tool is primarily beneficial when it comes to "negative SEO attacks," wherein a third party tries to harm a website's ranking by generating artificial, spammy backlinks typically prohibited by Google. By using the Disavow Tool, site owners can proactively protect their website from rather ruthless SEO tricks that others might employ (Siege Media, 2020).

It becomes the website owner's responsibility to identify these harmful links. This task often requires the use of SEO analytics tools like SEMRush or Google's Search Console, which provide complete profiles of a website's backlinks. Once these harmful links are identified, they can be included in a disavow file and uploaded to Google through the Disavow Tool.

However, Google cautions against the hasty use of the Disavow Tool, advising it as a "last resort" measure (Google Search Central, 2020). This is largely due to the potential for misuse – if used incorrectly, the Disavow Tool can cause more harm than good to a website's SEO efforts. Disavowing high-quality links, for instance, may inadvertently impact the site's performance. Hence, it becomes crucial to understand the nature of the backlinks thoroughly before taking any disavow action.

Overall, the Disavow Tool is a powerful, albeit complex, instrument in the SEO toolkit. It's a tool meant for expert hands, to be wielded with prudence and experience. For those serious about their website's SEO performance and health, mastering the Disavow Tool – understanding when and how to use it effectively – is an investment worth making.

Guest Blogging and its Impact on SEO

In the evolving world of online marketing, Search Engine Optimization (SEO) plays a pivotal role in garnering visibility and attracting organic traffic. One key strand of SEO strategy is guest blogging. It is a tactic used widely to enhance online reputation, reach a wider audience, and improve website ranking on search engine result pages (SERPs).

Guest blogging refers to the practice of contributing an chapter to another website or blog in the hope to build relationships, exposure, and most importantly, links (Summers, 2020). The reciprocal nature of this practice demonstrates its potential to mutually benefit both the guest author and the website hosting the guest content.

Participating in high-quality guest blogging can be a game changer in your SEO efforts. It offers both tangible and intangible benefits. Let's consider the tangible and direct SEO impacts first, with link building being primary among them.

Search engines like Google use links to discover new web pages and to help determine a page's ranking in its results. When you contribute an chapter to a well-established, high authority site, and link back to your website, it signals search engines about the legitimacy and authenticity of your site (Lewis, 2019). Backlinks from reputable websites bring credibility to your website significantly improving your website's SEO score.

Next, comes the intangible SEO benefits of guest blogging: exposure and authority. Exposure to a new audience can result in increased web traffic. Regular contributions to authoritative blogs enhance your image as an expert in your field, building your online authority (Neil Patel, 2021). Greater authority often leads to a higher trust factor, contributing to SEO in the long run.

Also, guest blogging improves your writing skills, forging healthy relationships with other bloggers and webmasters. It opens new doors for networking, collaboration, and building a brand.

Despite guest blogging's numerous benefits, one must avoid spammy tactics. It's critical to ensure high-quality content tailored for the audience of the host blog. Google frowns upon and penalizes manipulative link-building, which includes low-quality guest posting purely intended to gain backlinks (Google, 2020). Hence, the focus should be to add value through meaningful, high-quality content.

In conclusion, guest blogging plays a significant role in SEO strategy. It is an effective tool to earn valuable backlinks, broaden your audience, establish authority in your field, and ultimately boost your website's visibility on SERPs. However, a note of caution – it must be handled responsibly, ensuring quality over quantity to reap its full potential and avoid SEO penalties.

CHAPTER 6 - SOCIAL MEDIA AND LOCAL SEO

Role of Social Media in SEO…

In an era where digital marketing and online presence have become paramount, Search Engine Optimization (SEO) and Social Media have become intertwined. Platforms such as Facebook, LinkedIn, Instagram, or Twitter are indispensable instruments for brands that aim to create a considerable digital footprint. This chapter sheds light on the crucial role that Social Media plays in SEO.

While SEO is crucial for bringing organic traffic to websites, social media platforms function as vehicles that aid in driving this traffic. The relationship between the two can be aptly described via the 'Social SEO' model, which essentially indicates how interrelated they are in increasing a webpage's visibility on search engines (Patel, 2021).

One role that social media plays in SEO is driving referral traffic to websites. By sharing direct links to the website within social media posts, you can guide users towards the website, potentially garnering higher website traffic and ranking. Facebook alone accounts for over 30% of referral traffic (Borsetta, 2020), further emphasizing the significance of social media in SEO.

Furthermore, Brand Recognition and Brand Reputation are two critically significant factors in SEO. A strong social media presence can undoubtedly facilitate this when executed suitably. Enhancing your brand's reputation through regular, high-quality content on social media platforms can lead to users valuing your brand as a reliable source of information and improving your overall brand visibility.

Another notable effect of social media on SEO is Local SEO. When businesses utilize social media platforms to share location-specific posts or engage with localized community events, it increases their visibility on local searches. This approach is especially significant for local businesses looking to increase their online presence and credibility in their locality (Kumar, 2020).

Social Media also plays a pivotal role in fostering partnerships and collaborations. By networking with influential industry figures, businesses can enhance their brand's reputation and credibility. Furthermore, collaborations on social media often involve link-sharing, which can significantly drive traffic, hence affecting SEO.

Finally, the indirect influence of social signals on SEO cannot be underestimated. Although Google has clarified that social signals are not a direct ranking factor (Sullivan, 2018), reputed social media profiles with high user engagement tend to perform better in SERPs (Search Engine Result Pages). Therefore, a robust social media presence, with extensive shares, likes, and comments, can indirectly further SEO.

In conclusion, while Social Media may not directly affect SEO in terms of ranking algorithms, it undeniably serves as a considerable facilitator of SEO efforts. With a strategic approach and insightful utilization, Social Media can drive traffic, increase brand visibility and credibility, and indirectly bolster the website rankings on search engines.

How Social Signals Impact SEO

Search engine optimization (SEO) has long been recognized as a pivotal aspect of digital marketing. Over the years, various factors have been identified to impact SEO, and 'social signals' have recently emerged as a contributory component. Social signals refer to overall social media visibility and interactions that a piece of content receives such as shares, likes, comments, and views. This chapter seeks to elucidate the impact of these social signals on SEO.

Implementing successful SEO strategies involves optimizing your online presence to rank higher in search engine results. Social signals come into play here as they theoretically reflect the popularity of a website or its content. A prominent social media presence could potentially impact a website's search engine ranking.

Google's Matt Cutts, in a 2014 video, implied that social signals do not directly affect a website's ranking on Google's SERPs (Search Engine Results Pages). However, he further explicated that a high level of social activity could indirectly influence the organic visibility of a website, thus indirectly affecting SEO (Cutts, 2014).

For instance, shared content across diverse social media platforms results in consequent clicks through to the relevant website. More clicks infer more website traffic, a significantly important factor for SEO. Google algorithms identify these visits as a signal of relevance and popularity, which can potentially improve the website's ranking on the SERPs (Patel, 2017).

Moreover, the accumulation of substantial social signals could enhance a website's online visibility, creating an opportunity for backlinking. Other websites are more likely to link to popular, recognized content resulting in improved SEO, since backlinks are a primary driver of SEO.

Another essential point to note is that social signals aid in improving content indexing speed. A study by Moz demonstrated that popular chapters on Twitter and Facebook were likely to be indexed faster on Google. This means that content shared widely on social media would appear quicker on SERPs, enhancing the website's SEO.

While there may be varying viewpoints about the direct impact of social signals on SEO, its indirect influence cannot be disputed. High-level social activity invariably leads to increased web traffic and potential backlink opportunities, key elements for improving a website's SEO. The intrinsic link between social signals and SEO underscores the need for marketers to focus on maximizing social media engagements to boost SEO effectiveness.

In conclusion, while we might not have unequivocal corroboration for the direct impact of social signals on SEO, their indirect impact remains substantial. As such, a strategic and integrated approach to SEO must marshall the potential of social signals.

Importance of Positive Customer Reviews

The pivotal role of positive customer reviews in the era of social media cannot be overstated. In today's digitized world, more consumers turn to online reviews on various social platforms before making purchasing decisions. It is estimated that 90% of consumers read online reviews before visiting a business, and 88% of them trust online reviews as much as personal recommendations (BrightLocal, 2020). Social media, as a platform for these reviews, plays a significant role in shaping the perceptions and buying behaviors of consumers.

The presence of positive reviews on social media profiles directly influences the perceived trustworthiness of a company. Research shows that businesses with multiple positive reviews get 31% more business than those with few or no reviews (Womply, 2019). This is because positive reviews function as social proofs and act as persuasive testimonials that highlight the credibility of the business.

Additionally, positive customer reviews on social media amplify the visibility of a business. On platforms like Facebook and Google, a business with a high overall rating appears more frequently in search results. This increased visibility can lead to a boost in brand recognition and can result in higher organic website traffic.

Moreover, positive customer reviews on social media can have a significant effect on conversion rates. A study by Spiegel Research Center reports that displaying reviews can increase conversion rates by 270% (Spiegel, 2019). Positive customer reviews can help to eliminate any doubts a potential customer may have about a product or service, directly contributing to sales.

Further, customer reviews on social media can provide companies with valuable insights into their clientele. These reviews can highlight what a business is doing right and where improvements can be made. They provide an opportunity for companies to engage directly with their customers, fostering a sense of community and loyalty.

In conclusion, the necessity for positive customer reviews on social media is evident. They enhance the reputation, visibility, and conversion rates of a business, and offer vital insights into customer preferences. Businesses aiming for success in the digital marketplace should prioritize earning and promoting positive customer reviews on their social media platforms.

Local SEO and its Importance

Search Engine Optimization (SEO) is a pivotal aspect of modern digital marketing strategies. One of the most critical components of SEO is Local SEO (1). This facet of optimization targets location-specific queries, allowing businesses to compete within their local markets, thereby enhancing their visibility among local consumers.

Local SEO can be defined as the optimization of a website to improve visibility in searches with a local intent (2). This means that if a user searches for a specific service or product near their geographical location, optimized websites relating to the search will rank higher. For example, when a user searches for 'Italian restaurants near me,' websites of local Italian cuisine providers that have utilized Local SEO efficiently will appear in the top results.

The importance of Local SEO lies in its ability to provide specific, location-based results to users. With the rise of mobile technology, users frequently make location-specific searches. Local searches are often characterized by high purchase intent, as users typically have an immediate requirement for the goods or services they search for.

Local SEO focuses on several aspects to enhance a website's visibility. These include localization of website content, online reviews and ratings, local backlinks, and business listings in online directory listings, among others.

By optimizing these components, a business can significantly enhance its local online presence, ultimately driving more traffic and conversions.

Local businesses, including restaurants, salons, and retail stores, can particularly benefit from Local SEO. By visible to customers in their immediate geographical vicinity, they can increase footfall, build local recognition, and consequently, boost their revenue. A strong local SEO strategy allows independent businesses to compete with larger corporations by narrowing the competition to a local level.

The potential of Local SEO extends beyond brick-and-mortar businesses. Any organization looking to grow its presence in a specific geographical area can benefit from its incorporation in their digital marketing plan.

However, the successful implementation of Local SEO strategies necessitates expertise and intricate knowledge of SEO practices. It involves precise keyword targeting, comprehensive content optimization, high-quality link building, and a consistent online presence. Notably, the rapidly evolving nature of search engine algorithms necessitates regular updates and revisions of Local SEO strategies.

In conclusion, given the rising trend of location-specific searches and increased customer preference for local businesses, Local SEO has become a vital component of contemporary digital marketing. Businesses that are not focusing on Local SEO are missing out on a significant opportunity to grow their operations at a local level- regardless of their size or industry sector.

CHAPTER 7 - SEO TOOLS AND SOFTWARE

Introduction to SEO Tools

Search engine optimization (SEO) is a crucial aspect of online marketing. It entails optimizing your website to make it more visible on search engines, which increases traffic and potentially leads to higher conversion rates. The complexity of SEO requires the use of various tools to achieve the best results. These SEO tools play an essential role in stirring the success of internet marketing and are thus necessary for every online business. This chapter introduces the concept of SEO tools, their relevance, and a few examples of the most commonly used ones.

SEO tools are software designed to help you improve your website's search engine ranking. They provide information or perform tasks that would otherwise require an enormous amount of time and expertise. Some tools will analyze your website and provide specific recommendations for improving your site's ranking on search engine results pages (SERPs). While others will monitor your site's performance and report any issues that might hurt your search engine rankings.

There are several categories of SEO tools, each serving a specific purpose in the optimization process. One such category is keyword research tools. These tools help you identify, research, and select keywords that your target audience uses when searching for your products or services. Examples include Google Keyword Planner and SEMrush.

Another notable category is on-page SEO tools. These tools help with optimizing individual web pages in ways that make them rank higher and earn more relevant traffic in search engines. They analyze your pages, provide real-time feedback on your SEO efforts and identify areas that need improvement. Yoast SEO and Moz Pro are popular tools in this category.

Link building tools form another category and are crucial for off-page SEO. These ensure that you get high-quality backlinks from relevant and authoritative websites. Tools like Ahrefs and Majestic are designed to offer complete link building and backlink management solutions.

Lastly, technical SEO tools are used to check website issues affecting your ranking. They help in finding broken links, detecting duplicate content, or checking page loading speed. Google Search Console and Screaming Frog SEO Spider are examples of technical SEO tools.

SEO tools should not be neglected because they can offer tremendous benefits. They save time, provide a competitive edge, and give insights into your competitors' strategies. Additionally, they can help you uncover opportunities that you might not have identified, and give you various ways to refine and monitor the performance of your SEO strategy.

In conclusion, SEO tools are integral in streamlining your SEO efforts. They help in keyword research, on-page optimization, link building, and diagnosing technical website issues. By understanding the essence of these tools, you are bound to make significant strides in your online marketing campaign.

Google Analytics

Google Analytics is an invaluable digital analytics software owned and managed by Google that offers fundamental insights into website and user interaction data, serving as an integral tool for marketing (The New York Times, 2018). With the aim to determine the efficacy of online campaigns and understand user browsing patterns, Google Analytics is a dynamic tool that aids businesses in adjusting their strategies by providing pertinent data about their online presence.

The free-to-use tool, Google Analytics, is profoundly transformative, breaking down complex datasets into an easily comprehendible format through comprehensive, tailor-made reports(Digital Marketing Institute, 2017). With its innovative approach, businesses can assess universal data about the number of users on their domain, session duration, bounce rates, and pages per session, allowing for accurate evaluation and prompt modification of their webpage performance.

A salient feature of Google Analytics is its ability to furnish goal-setting facilities. Ranging from the duration of sessions to the number of downloads, businesses can set any goal relevant to their operations and track attainment against these goals (Google Analytics Help, 2021). Furthermore, Google Analytics also bestows users with real-time visitor data, which may offer insights into the efficacy of a business's latest online marketing campaign.

The power of Google Analytics extends to its E-commerce tracking functionality, making it an essential tool for E-retailers and businesses with online sales platforms (G2,

2019). With E-commerce tracking, businesses can scrutinize user purchase data, product or service performance, transaction details, and revenues, impacting timely decision-making and goal revisions.

Google Analytics' advanced segments functionality enables businesses to create subsets of their traffic, providing valuable data on user behavior, conversion rate optimizations, and revenue (webfx, 2020). It helps filter data obtained from different segments, enabling a specific focus on various user groups.

Another remarkable feature of Google Analytics is its multichannel funnels, which provide insights into the entire customer journey- the different online paths customers take before finalizing a purchase or conversion. This furthers understanding of the impact of different marketing channels and their contribution to overall sales and conversions, which is fundamental for businesses prioritizing multi-faceted digital marketing strategies (Supermetrics, 2020).

Despite its numerous benefits, potential users should be aware of the limitations of Google Analytics, such as data sampling issues, difficulties in tracking across domains, and data accuracy challenges caused by ad-blockers and cookie-less browsing (SearchEngineJournal, 2019). Therefore, it is crucial to leverage Google Analytics in combination with other data and marketing analytics tools to gain a comprehensive view of online performance and customer behavior.

In conclusion, the robust capabilities of Google Analytics make it a staple tool for businesses striving for digital marketing success. It provides critical insights into customer behavior, digital campaign performance, and website interaction data, allowing businesses to finely tune their strategies and tread a path towards increased online success.

Google Search Console

Google Search Console (GSC) is an indispensable tool developed by Google to allow website administrators to monitor and manage their website's online presence in Google's search results. With the effective use of this tool, website owners can gain valuable insights and improve their website's visibility on the Google search engine results page (SERP). This chapter aims to provide a comprehensive overview of the Google Search Console and its potential applications (Google Support, 2021).

The Google Search Console is a platform that allows you to understand how Google and its users view your website. With GSC, you can submit new content for crawling or remove content you don't want to be shown in search results. Additionally, it enables you to monitor your site for errors, security issues, and optimization opportunities to ensure that your website is fully indexed and visibly present in search engine results (Chavda, 2019).

One of the key features of Google Search Console is the performance report. This feature provides data about your website's performance on Google Search, including clicks, impressions, click-through rates (CTR), and the site's position on SERP. By analyzing this data, website owners can understand how well the site is performing and where improvements may be needed (Google Support, 2021).

Another valuable tool within the Search Console is the URL inspection tool. This feature allows website administrators to check specific URLs on the website to view their crawl, index, and serving status directly from the

Google index. It provides detailed information, including the last crawl date, any indexing errors, and the URL's canonical status, ensuring that URLs are properly indexed by Google (GSC, Google Support, 2021).

The Coverage report feature in GSC shows the indexing state of all pages on the site that Google has visited. This tool can be beneficial to identify potential indexing issues and rectify them, leading to improved visibility on the search engine result page (Google Support, 2021).

The Google Search Console also hosts several other tools including, sitemaps, mobile usability, AMP status, and structured data. All these features combined make the Google Search Console a comprehensive platform for managing a website's online presence in Google's search results (Google Support, 2021).

In conclusion, the Google Search Console is a powerful tool that every website administrator should utilize. With its impressive array of functionalities -- from submitting and checking crawl, index, and serving urls to receiving alerts for issues and performance analytics -- Google Search Console plays a pivotal role in the optimization of a website for better SERP visibility.

SEMrush

SEMrush is a versatile and cutting-edge search engine optimization (SEO) tool. Over the years, it has garnered acclaim as an invaluable resource for bolstering online marketing campaigns, elevating website traffic, and improving overall SEO performance. SEMrush offers comprehensive insights into various key aspects of digital marketing such as pay-per-click (PPC) advertising, social media, and content and PR, to enable businesses to optimize their strategies and maximize outcomes

(SEMrush, n.d.).

One important feature of SEMrush is its domain analysis tool. This aspect of SEMrush is indispensable for comparing your own website with competitors. It generates actionable data regarding organic search, paid search, and backlinks. The data gleaned can then be employed to optimize your website and enhance its visibility in search engine results pages (SERPs) (Adespresso by Hootsuite, 2021).

SEMrush's keyword research feature is another noteworthy aspect. It provides key data on the value of specific keywords, such as their volume, number of results, and trend. Moreover, it offers information on related keywords and phrase matches, which can be extremely advantageous for improving a website's SEO performance. By using this tool, businesses can strategically select keywords to enhance their online visibility (Puranam, 2020).

Digital marketers immensely value the site audit tool of SEMrush. The feature, quick in identifying issues that may hamper a website's visibility in search results, also provides recommendations for improvements. Regularly conducting site audits can significantly enhance a website's SEO performance, making it more searchable and user-friendly (SEMrush, n.d.).

Let's not overlook SEMrush's gap analysis tool. This feature allows businesses to compare their keyword portfolios with those of competitors. Using this tool can help businesses identify underutilized keywords that provide an opportunity for increased website traffic. Furthermore, it facilitates the identification of top-performing keywords utilized by competitors, thereby inspiring new keyword strategies (Puranam, 2020).

Finally, the social media toolkit of SEMrush can help companies execute and analyze their social media campaigns. The toolkit provides valuable insights into other businesses' social media strategies, thus providing inspiration and guidance for a company's own approach (Adespresso by Hootsuite, 2021).

In conclusion, SEMrush is a truly versatile SEO tool with myriad features that offer valuable insights to help optimize various aspects of digital marketing. It is, therefore, an invaluable resource for businesses looking to maximize reach and visibility in the digital sphere.

Moz

Moz is a highly recognized and influential software-as-a-service (SaaS) company that specializes in search engine optimization (SEO) tools. Established in 2004 by Rand Fishkin and Gillian Muessig, it quickly became a leading force in the SEO industry with its rich suite of SEO tools, educational resources, and marketing analytics solutions (Built In, n.d.).

Moz's core offerings revolve around inbound marketing and marketing analytics services, but it's perhaps more renowned for its contribution to advancing SEO. Moz offers a set of tools collectively known as MOZ Pro, making it an instrumental resource for SEO professionals who are keen on improving a website's visibility, driving organic traffic, and gaining insight into their competitors' strategies (Moz, n.d.).

The MOZ Pro suite encompasses several integral components, including a Keyword Explorer, Rank Tracker, Site Crawler, and On-Page Optimizer. The Keyword Explorer tool assists marketers in identifying the most effective keywords for their SEO strategy, whereas the Rank Tracker provides data on a website's search engine rankings for targeted keywords (Moz, n.d.).

The Site Crawler is instrumental in identifying SEO issues that could negatively impact the website's visibility. The On-Page Optimizer, on the other hand, aids in analyzing and optimizing individual pages of the website to improve their SEO scores (Moz, n.d.).

In addition to Moz Pro, MozLocal is another significant offering that is designed to ease the digital marketing efforts of local businesses. It improves online visibility for local businesses by ensuring their business listings are accurate, consistent, and visible across the web (Moz, n.d.). Moz substantiates its significant contributions to SEO with a commitment to educating its clientele and general users. The Moz Blog, for instance, is a renowned SEO resource that regularly publishes insightful chapters and advice on SEO strategies and trends (Moz, n.d.).

At its core, Moz exemplifies an integrated SEO platform offering comprehensive tools and resources to business owners, digital marketers, and SEO professionals. Moz culture thrives on transparency, generosity, and fun; and this typifies their approach in striving to enable users to achieve their SEO goals, thus simplifying the complexities of SEO.

Moz's potent combination of technology and search-marketing expertise empowers users to better comprehend SEO processes. As a result, they can yield greater returns from their SEO investments and fortify their digital marketing strategies.

In sum, Moz has revolutionized the way businesses and marketers approach SEO. At its core, it's not just a tool but a robust platform that bridges the gap between search engine algorithms and user-friendly SEO practices.

Exploiting SEO Automation Software

Search Engine Optimization (SEO) has played a critical role in enhancing digital marketing strategies to increase online visibility. As businesses continue to navigate the digital marketing landscape, the use of SEO automation software is becoming prevalent to manage complex SEO tasks efficiently. The automation of SEO processes is not about replacing human involvement but maximizing efficiency and effectiveness. This chapter explores the concept of SEO automation software and how businesses can harness its power to improve their online presence.

SEO automation software refers to tools explicitly designed to simplify and automate repetitive SEO tasks (1). These software systems come with features that enable businesses to automate tasks such as keyword research, link building, website audits, rank tracking, and competitor analysis. SEO automation is predominantly crucial in a digital marketing ecosystem formulated on data-driven decision-making processes (2).

The use of SEO automation software offers several benefits. Firstly, by leveraging this strategy, businesses can save both time and resources. With the software handling repetitive tasks, the SEO team can focus more on complex strategic tasks, including refining the SEO strategy, experimenting with new SEO techniques, and content creation. This can increase the efficiency and effectiveness of SEO efforts (3).

Secondly, SEO automation software offers reliable and consistent data which can be critical in making strategic decisions. Data accuracy is more critical than ever in SEO, and automation software can provide this consistency and reliability. Accurate data helps understand the impact of SEO strategy on online visibility and make modifications as required.

Lastly, SEO automation software offers scalability, a key component in the rapid progression of SEO strategies. As the business grows, its SEO requirements also increase. Automating SEO tasks can help in managing the growing SEO workload (4).

Despite these benefits, exploiting SEO automation software must be a well-thought-out process. Businesses should start by automating tasks that are time-consuming and repetitive, such as rank tracking and link building. This would free up considerable time for SEO professionals to concentrate on tasks that require more strategy and creativity.

Furthermore, while automating SEO tasks, businesses should ensure not to over-rely on the software. While it helps immensely in handling repetitive tasks, automating tasks requiring human inaccuracy might lead to lower efficiency. Therefore, finding the right balance in automation is critical for a successful SEO strategy (5).

In conclusion, SEO automation software could be a game-changer for businesses looking to enhance their online visibility. By automating specific tasks, businesses can streamline their SEO strategies and, as a result, enjoy improved overall effectiveness in their digital marketing campaigns.

CHAPTER 8 - MEASURING AND MONITORING SEO RESULTS

KPIs and Metrics for SEO Progress

Search Engine Optimization (SEO) strategies play a significant role in enhancing your online visibility, fostering higher brand recognition, and significantly driving business growth. However, the evaluation of your SEO efforts' effectiveness is equally crucial for continuous improvement and achieving desired outcomes. Consequently, you must understand the Key Performance Indicators (KPIs) and metrics for SEO progress to track your success (Harris, 2019).

Search rankings, organic traffic, backlinks, and keyword performance are among the mainstream KPIs to gauge your SEO effort's effectiveness. Metrics, on the other hand, are quantifiable measures that relay how well your KPIs are performing. A deep understanding of these parameters can guide future content strategies, giving businesses an edge over their competition.

Top Search Ranking is an essential KPI for measuring SEO progress. Simply put, the higher your website appears on search engine result pages (SERPs), the greater your chances of attracting potential customers. Notwithstanding, achieving a top spot might not always lead to higher traffic if your content doesn't align with user intent (Patel, 2020).

Organic Traffic is another SEO progress indicator. Organic traffic refers to the users that land on your website through unpaid search results instead of paid advertisements. Higher organic traffic often corresponds to better SEO practices and is deemed a good indicator of effective keyword usage, backlinks, and high-quality content.

An increased number of Backlinks, links that point to your website from other websites, signifies popularity and credibility, both vital factors for improving your SEO ranking. A metric to monitor for backlinks would be the number of unique domains linking to your website, which search engines consider as votes towards your credibility (Fishkin, 2018).

Keyword Performance is an indicator of how well you have optimized your website's content with specific words or phrases relevant to your product or service. Metrics to observe for keyword performance include Keyword Ranking, which shows your site's position for specific keywords, and SERP Visibility, denoting the percentage of impressions your website gets based on those keywords.

Bounce Rate, while not a KPI, is a vital SEO progress metric. It represents the percentage of visitors that navigate away from your website after viewing only one page. A lower bounce rate implies that users find your content engaging and useful.

Additionally, Click-Through Rate (CTR) is the ratio of users who clicked on a specific link relative to the number of total users who viewed the page. If your CTR is low, it could indicate that your titles and descriptions are not compelling or relevant (Google Search Central, n.d.).

To recapitulate, understanding KPIs and metrics for SEO progress is crucial for optimizing your digital marketing strategy and ensuring you achieve your business growth objectives. By keeping track of these indicators regularly, you can take informed decisions, implement appropriate measures and enhance your website's SEO performance.

Using Analytics for SEO Tracking

Title: Utilizing Analytics for Effective SEO Tracking

Introduction

Search Engine Optimization (SEO) plays a significant role in digital marketing. Ensuring that websites rank higher in search engine results pages boosts visibility and increases organic traffic. To accurately ascertain the effectiveness of your SEO strategies, it is vital to utilize analytics for tracking (Patel, 2019). Analytics tools provide vital insights into the performance of your website, enabling you to optimize your digital marketing strategies further.

The Importance of Analytics in SEO

Analytics is highly crucial for SEO due to its ability to provide extensive site performance data. Once you understand the sources of your website's traffic, the pages that attract more visitors, or patterns in user behavior, it becomes easier to devise effective SEO strategies. With analytics, companies can pinpoint the elements of their SEO strategies that work and those that need improvement. Moreover, it allows continuous monitoring of these strategies, facilitating quick adjustments when necessary.

Using Analytics for Keyword Tracking

Keywords are essential in SEO, which means their tracking is pivotal. Through analytics, you can track the performance of specific keywords in terms of driving traffic, leading to conversions and improving your search engine ranking (Enge, Spencer, & Stricchiola, 2015). This information aids in fine-tuning your keyword strategies, empowering you to better utilize high-performing keywords and drop or improve on low-performing ones. Google Analytics, in particular, gives insights on the keywords users are utilizing to find your webpages, paving the way for more targeted content creation.

Analytics for Link Tracking

Backlink tracking and monitoring is yet another critical aspect of SEO that benefits significantly from the use of analytics. A backlink is a hyperlink from one website linking back to your site. The more quality backlinks your site has, the higher its chances of ranking better in search engine results. Analytic tools, such as SEMRush or Moz, can help you monitor your backlink profile and identify potentially harmful links that could negatively affect your search engine rankings (Cooper, 2014).

Analytics for User Engagement

User engagement is paramount in SEO strategy. High engagement levels on your website increase the likelihood of higher search engine rankings. Analytic tools can help track user engagement by providing information such as bounce rate, average session duration, and pages per session. These metrics can offer insights into how engaging your content is, enabling you to make appropriate modifications to improve user experience and, subsequently, SEO rankings.

Conclusion

The integration of analytics in SEO tracking offers an unprecedented scope of understanding and improving your site's performance. It allows businesses to create data-driven SEO strategies, ensuring their content aligns with user preferences, interests, and search patterns. While data analytics may seem daunting, the insights it provides are invaluable in the world of digital marketing, fostering sustained growth and success.

Case Study: A Successful SEO Strategy

The world today is experiencing a digital age, wherein online presence is significantly essential for businesses. It is in this context that Search Engine Optimization (SEO) plays a vital role in enhancing online visibility and traffic. This chapter presents a case study that showcases a successful SEO strategy implemented by a small-scale e-commerce firm, which resulted in a considerable traffic increase and improved search engine rankings.

The e-commerce firm wanted to optimize its website to increase organic traffic and gain a competitive edge in the ever-dynamic online market landscape. The firm thus adopted a holistic SEO strategy involving SEO audit, keyword research, content creation, link building, and technical SEO.

Initially, the firm conducted an SEO audit to evaluate the site's current performance and identify areas requiring improvement. The process involved analyzing site structure, meta-tags, page-loading speed, mobile-friendliness, and backlinks, among other SEO metrics, to determine any existing gaps (Patel, 2020).

Next was the ever-crucial stage of keyword research. The firm used tools like Google Keyword Planner, SEMRush, and Ahrefs to identify relevant, high-volume keywords with low competition. They focused on long-tail keywords as these benefited the website's ranking, providing less competition and a more targeted audience.

Content creation took center-stage as the core of SEO strategy. The firm prioritized high-quality, unique, and keyword-optimized content for blog posts, landing pages, and product descriptions. This initiative presented an opportunity to incorporate the researched keywords while ensuring the content was engaging and adding value to the readers (Fishkin, 2021).

Link building was another cornerstone of this SEO strategy. The firm executed a comprehensive link building campaign, which involved creating high-quality, shareable content, guest posting, and leveraging social media platforms to earn backlinks.

Lastly, the firm did not overlook the importance of technical SEO. They ensured a mobile-friendly design, fast page-loading speed, and an intuitive site structure that positively impacted the user experience, indirectly contributing to SEO.

Within six months, the e-commerce firm experienced a 75% increase in organic traffic, a reduction in bug rate by 60%, and an advancement in the rankings on Search Engine Results Page (SERP) for their targeted keywords. This case study underscores the crucial role that a well-planned and executed SEO strategy plays in enhancing a website's visibility and boosting online traffic.

This instance emphasizes that SEO is not an overnight magic spell but requires a strategic, well-planned, and dedicated approach. Persistence and continual optimization adjustments according to changing algorithms and search trends are critical in any successful SEO strategy.

In conclusion, the SEO strategy implemented by this e-commerce firm exhibits how an amalgamation of adequate research, creating winning content, and technical efficiency can create a significant impact on driving organic traffic and improving SERP rankings.

CHAPTER 9 - FUTURE OF SEO

Emerging Trends in SEO (Voice Search, AI)

Search engine optimization (SEO), the craft of increasing a website's visibility in search engine results pages (SERPs), is a dynamic field subject to rapid changes. Two conspicuous developments poised to reshape the future of SEO are voice search and artificial intelligence (AI). As touted by industry insiders, these trends present a thrilling, albeit slightly daunting, prospect for digital marketers and SEO specialists.

Voice Search

With the advent and proliferation of voice-activated technologies like Amazon's Alexa, Apple's Siri, and Google's Assistant, voice search is swiftly becoming a mainstream method of online information-seeking. Unlike traditional text searches, voice searches are typically longer, more conversational, and framed as direct questions. According to PwC, around 71% of consumers prefer using voice search to typing their queries, thus underscoring the need for SEO strategies to adapt accordingly (1).

Such adaptation necessitates a focus on long-tail keywords and development of content that directly answers users' questions. Additionally, it is incumbent upon businesses to ensure their websites are mobile-friendly and possess fast load times, as most voice searches occur on mobile devices. Moreover, optimizing for 'near me' searches is crucial, given their high prevalence in voice search queries.

Artificial Intelligence (AI)

Perhaps equally significant in transforming the SEO environment is AI, with Google's machine learning algorithm, RankBrain, a case in point. AI algorithms analyze the way users interact with search results, thereby fortifying the accuracy of Google's query results.

Ensuring SEO strategies align with AI's growing influence involves creating quality content that resonates with the target audience. In this context, quality content means content that is informative, engaging, and provides real value to readers. Websites churning out such content are more likely to generate positive user engagement signals, translating into better SERP rankings courtesy of AI algorithms.

Businesses must stay vigilant about these emerging trends and incorporate them into their SEO strategies. A keen awareness and understanding of voice search and AI trends will be vital for businesses to maintain a competitive edge in the increasingly crowded digital marketplace.

In conclusion, voice search and AI are no longer novelty pursuits on the fringes of SEO. They are rapidly becoming central to optimizing business websites for maximum search visibility and, ultimately, customer acquisition and retention.

How to Stay Up-to-Date with SEO Trends

Search Engine Optimization (SEO) has proven to be a significant tool in the digital marketing world. However, it is ever-changing, and marketers need to stay updated with the latest trends to remain competitive. Here are some of the ways for digital marketers to keep abreast of the latest SEO trends.

First, subscribing to credible SEO newsletters is an ideal way to stay updated on SEO trends. Websites like Search Engine Land, SEMRush, and Moz publish regular SEO newsletters providing updates on the latest developments in SEO (Kissmetrics, 2020). These newsletters cover everything from algorithm changes to new, in-depth guides on specific SEO topics.

Secondly, attending SEO webinars and virtual conferences is a good way to learn about the latest changes in SEO. These seminars often have experts in the field who share their insights and experiences. They cover subjects like the changing landscape of SEO, new tools, and techniques, as well as case studies on successful SEO strategies.

Following industry experts on social media platforms such as LinkedIn and Twitter can be beneficial. Many SEO professionals such as Rand Fishkin, Neil Patel, and Danny Sullivan frequently share their thoughts and insights about the latest SEO trends on these platforms (Kissmetrics, 2020).

Reading SEO-related blogs can help keep one's knowledge of SEO updated. Websites such as Moz and Search Engine Journal continually update their blogs with SEO information. They cover a wide variety of topics, from basic SEO knowledge to in-depth explorations of specific SEO concepts. These blogs also often feature articles written by industry experts in the field of SEO (Kissmetrics, 2020).

Listening to SEO podcasts is a productive way to stay current on SEO trends during commute hours or while multitasking. Podcasts like "The Search Engine Journal Show" and "The SEO Podcast - Unknown Secrets of Internet Marketing" regularly have SEO experts share their knowledge, advice as well their update about the industry. Lastly, considering an SEO training course can also be beneficial. Many SEO training courses, including those offered by Moz and SEMRush, keep their curriculum updated to reflect the latest trends in SEO. Taking these courses not only provides a structured approach to learning SEO but also ensures that your SEO knowledge remains current (SEMRush, 2020).

Staying updated in SEO is a continuous process, and it can be quite tough because of its dynamic nature. However, by leveraging these resources mentioned above, one can ensure that they are ahead of their game in understanding and applying the latest SEO trends.

As marketing professionals, we must remember that the goal of SEO is not simply to rank highly on search engine results but to provide users with relevant and high-quality content. Keeping this goal in mind will guide us as we adapt to the evolving SEO trends.

Predictions for SEO Future

Search Engine Optimization (SEO) can be regarded as an ever-evolving digital marketing strategy that faces modifications regularly. Over the past years, there have been constant improvements in digital and Internet culture, transforming SEO's trajectory. So, what should we expect in the near future concerning SEO? In this chapter, we highlight and discuss some trends and predictions for the future of SEO.

Firstly, mobile search optimization will be a dominant focal point. With a surge in mobile usage across the globe, search engines like Google have shifted emphasis towards mobile-first indexing (Bock, 2019). This means the mobile version of a website will predominantly be considered for indexing and ranking purposes. Websites that fail to meet mobile usability expectations may observe ranking drops in search engine results.

Secondly, artificial intelligence (AI) and machine learning are playing an increasing role in SEO. AI has already started revolutionizing SEO with tools such as Google's RankBrain, an algorithm learning AI system, aiding with processing search results (Ali, 2021). As AI continues to evolve, so too will SEO strategies, such as keyword research, content marketing, and back-linking.

Voice search is another trend predicted to proliferate. With the advancement in technology and increased usage of Siri, Google Assistant, and Alexa, voice search is fast becoming a mainstream search method. As a result, SEO strategies are expected to optimize for natural language search, an approach that utilizes conversational queries instead of keyword-focused ones (McGinnis, 2020).

Fourthly, user experience (UX) is deemed to gain more importance. Google aims to enhance web users' experience by developing its algorithm to prioritize websites that guarantee a smooth, enjoyable user journey. The incorporation of Core Web Vitals into Google's ranking algorithm in May 2021 is a significant step towards this direction (Sullivan, 2020).

Finally, local SEO is expected to be prioritized even more. With "near me" searches becoming increasingly common, businesses need to enhance their local SEO efforts to be visible to potential customers within their locality (Ali, 2021).

In conclusion, the future of SEO lies in its adaptability towards technological advancements and changing user behavior. SEO strategies ought to be flexible and innovative, considering the changing dynamics of search engine algorithms, technological advancements, and user expectations and behaviors.

CONCLUSION

Recap of SEO Importance

Search Engine Optimization (SEO) remains an integral part of the digital marketing landscape. This chapter provides a comprehensive recap of the principal importance of SEO in today's digital age.

SEO refers to the process of enhancing a website to make it more visible for relevant searches on search engines like Bing, Yahoo, and particularly Google (Search Engine Land, 2021). A well-optimized website can garner more attention and, ultimately, generate more traffic, leads, and conversions, which are pivotal for the success of any online venture.

The primary importance of SEO arises from its role in enhancing visibility and ranking. Research shows that the majority of online experiences begin with a search engine, and a vast proportion of traffic goes to sites listed on the first page of the search results (Chitika, 2013). Evidently, higher-ranking sites enjoy an enormous advantage over their lower-ranking counterparts, emphasizing the significance of a well-deployed SEO strategy.

Besides the role in visibility and ranking, SEO is a crucial tool for building credibility and trust. This is because search engines are designed to promote authoritative and relevant content. By executing good SEO practices, like producing quality content, maintaining user-friendly site architecture, and demonstrating backlink profiles, online businesses can climb up the SERPs (Search Engine Results Pages) and establish themselves as credible sources of information (Forbes, 2017).

SEO is additionally significant for its contribution to the user experience. An integral aspect of SEO involves making a website easy for both users and search engine bots to understand. This usually involves ensuring the website is mobile-friendly, decreasing loading times, and having an intuitive site navigation — features that significantly improve the overall experience for users (Search Engine Journal, 2020).

Last but not least, SEO offers an invaluable advantage over the competition. In the highly competitive digital marketplace, having a robust SEO strategy can be the difference between being visible to potential customers or being overlooked. By continually keeping up with changes in search engine algorithms and consumer search habits, businesses can maintain a competitive edge by ensuring they maintain high visibility and relevancy where it matters most.

In conclusion, SEO is a multifaceted tool of immense importance in today's digital age. It plays a significant role in enhancing online visibility and ranking, building credibility, improving the user experience, and offering a competitive edge. Thus, a well-strategized and properly executed SEO strategy remains non-negotiable for any online business hoping to thrive in the digital marketplace.

Emphasis on Continuous Learning in SEO

In the ever-dynamic world of Search Engine Optimization (SEO), there is an undoubted emphasis on continuous learning to maintain success and a competitive edge. SEO is a crucial aspect of online marketing that centers around optimizing a website to improve visibility on search engine results pages (SERPs). With search engines continually tweaking their algorithms to enhance the experience of the user and make search results as relevant as possible, those in the SEO industry must be on their toes, always ready to adapt (O'Brien, 2019).

Admittedly, the constant shifts and updates can seem overwhelming, but they serve as opportunities to learn and fine-tune skills progressively. Continuous learning in SEO involves keeping up to date with the latest SEO trends, understanding changes to search engine algorithms, exploring new tools and technologies, and learning from best practices across multiple industries (O'Neil, 2018).

Understanding search engine algorithms and how they react to various website factors is integral in optimizing a website's ranking. Google, the largest and most popular search engine, is known to adjust its algorithm frequently. In fact, in 2018, Google reported an astounding 3,234 updates — an average of almost 9 per day (Brodsky, 2020). Continuous learning helps SEO specialists to keep up with these changes and apply relevant adjustments to their strategies.

There's also an abundance of emerging tools and technologies in the SEO sphere. Knowledge of such resources, like Google Analytics, Google Search Console, SEMrush, and Moz Pro, can boost one's ability to collect and analyze SEO data, inform strategies and identify areas for improvement (Fishkin, 2019).

Learning from best practices across different industries is another facet of continuous learning in SEO. Although each industry will have unique SEO challenges and objectives, there are nuggets of wisdom that can be gleaned from how others have approached similar challenges. Such cross-industry learning can foster innovative thinking and approach to SEO.

Moreover, the benefits of continuous learning in SEO are numerous. It helps professionals stay relevant in the ever-evolving digital landscape and ensure they are always equipped with the right knowledge and expertise to optimize websites effectively. They gain insights into new trends, techniques, and best practices that can enhance their SEO strategy. Through this constant development, individuals and businesses will have an edge in the highly competitive online market.

To conclude, the emphasis on continuous learning in SEO cannot be overstated. As search engine algorithms become more complex and refined, their understanding calls for a consistent commitment to learning and development. The dynamic nature of SEO necessitates a willingness to engage in continual learning, not only as a means to stay relevant but also as an avenue to drive innovation, improve strategies, and ultimately, enhance online visibility.

Final Thoughts

SEO, or Search Engine Optimization, is a digital marketing methodology that plays an integral role in elevating a business's online visibility. It's a concept that examines search engine algorithms and the human visitor's behavior to get a website's web page to rank higher on major search engines (Godwin, 2020).

Businesses invest heavily in SEO to build a strong web presence, and it has become a relatively unavoidable aspect of attracting online visitors. One of the reasons for popularity is that, when compared with other digital marketing plans, SEO tactics provide a superior Return on Investment (ROI).

Keyword optimization is an essential step of the SEO overall strategy. Incorporating relevant keywords in your website content helps your website rank higher on search engine result pages (SERPs) (Nelms, 2021). But, keyword stuffing is negatively regarded, giving websites a spam-like feel. Instead, it is more effective to utilize long-tail keywords to help your website rank for more specific, low-competition searches.

Link-building is the spine of SEO, allowing search engines to notice the existence and work of your page. Good content paired with strong backlinks from reputable sites helps boost domain authority and improve your website's ranking (Clay, 2020).

Local SEO is a significantly influential factor for businesses that operate in specific geographical areas. With local SEO in place, they can get their services and products to show up in localized search results, thus targeting potential customers within their defined operating area.

Another important aspect of SEO is mobile optimization. Increasingly, people are using mobile devices to browse the web, and search engines like Google make 'mobile-friendliness' a ranking factor. Therefore, to stay competitive, it is crucial for websites to be responsive, that is, designed to adjust and look good on any device (O'Neill, 2019).

The role of social media in SEO should not be underestimated either. Powerful social signals can greatly encourage a brand's search results and provide both direct and indirect benefits to a website's visibility.

Although SEO efforts take time to manifest results, the reward is worth the wait. Consistency, patience, and correct selection of tactics form the backbone of a successful SEO campaign. No website can gain real-time overnight results on SERPs. Therefore, one key rule is to consistently strive for improvement, be patient, and be persistent.

Always remember, just like Rome was not built in a day; neither can a website's SEO. With google constantly changing and updating algorithms, the SEO landscape is always evolving, thereby making it necessary for businesses to adapt and change their SEO strategies accordingly.

That said, let's not underestimate the importance of keeping up with these changes and constantly improving the SEO strategies to adapt to the forever-evolving digital landscape.

In conclusion, the success of any online business heavily depends on how effectively they can master SEO strategies. Search engines are the primary method of navigation for most Internet users, which keeps SEO an integral aspect of the modern digital ecosystem.

Table of contents

Glossary

List of Common SEO Terms and Definitions

In the world of digital marketing, understanding Search Engine Optimization (SEO) is fundamental. SEO is the process of enhancing a website's visibility on search engines, thereby driving organic traffic to the site[1]. Here is a glossary of some of the most common SEO terms and definitions to help you better understand this vital field.

1) SEO: Search Engine Optimization involves tailoring a website's content and design to rank higher in search engine results. It increases the quantity and quality of online traffic and enhances brand exposure.

2) SERP: The Search Engine Results Page displays the search results a person receives after querying a search engine. High-ranking websites appear at the top of the SERP.

3) Organic Traffic: This is the number of visitors that land on a page naturally without being driven there by paid advertising. SEO aims to increase organic traffic, as it indicates the source material's relevance and appeal[2].

4) Keywords: These are the phrases or terms users enter into a search engine. By including relevant keywords in the content, websites can rank higher in search results.

5) Meta-tags: These are HTML tags used to identify a web page's key topics to search engines. They provide concise, information-rich summaries of the website's content.

6) Backlinks: These are external hyperlinks from one page to another website. High-quality backlinks from reputable domains can significantly improve a website's SEO.

7) Page Rank: Google's algorithm to rank webpages based on relevance and authority. Not to be confused with SERP ranking, which involves additional factors like user experience and content quality.

8) Anchor text: The clickable text in a hyperlink usually uses SEO-friendly keyword phrases.

9) Canonical URL: The preferred URL when multiple versions of a page are available. It helps avoid duplicate content issues affecting SEO negatively.

10) Robots.txt: A text file web servers use to instruct search engine crawlers on how to crawl and index the site's content.

This list is by no means exhaustive, but understanding these basic SEO terms is vital to any digital marketing initiative or online business's success. SEO has the potential to provide high returns when done right, so understanding these terms can make a substantial difference in your digital strategy[3].